CODING UNPLUGGED

CODING WITH NATURE

GETTING KID-CODERS OFF THE SCREEN AND ON THEIR FEET!

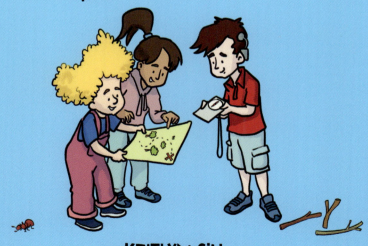

BY KAITLYN SIU
ILLUSTRATED BY DAVE SMITH

Gareth Stevens
PUBLISHING

WARNING

We recommend adult supervision at all times while doing the activities in this book. Always be aware that craft materials may contain allergens, so check the packaging for allergens if there is a risk of an allergic reaction. Anyone with a known allergy must avoid these.
- Wear an apron and cover surfaces.
- Tie back long hair.
- Ask an adult for help with cutting.
- Check materials for allergens.

Please visit our website, www.garethstevens.com. For a free color catalog of all our high-quality books, call toll free 1-800-542-2595 or fax 1-877-542-2596.

Cataloging-in-Publication Data
Names: Siu, Kaitlyn, author. | Smith, Dave, illustrator.
Title: Coding with nature / Kaitlyn Siu , illustrated by Dave Smith.
Description: Buffalo, NY : Gareth Stevens Publishing, 2026. | Series: Coding unplugged | Includes glossary and index.
Identifiers: ISBN 9781482473759 (pbk.) | ISBN 9781482473766 (library bound) | ISBN 9781482473773 (ebook)
Subjects: LCSH: Computer programming--Juvenile literature. | Coding theory--Juvenile literature. | Nature--Juvenile literature.
Classification: LCC QA76.6115 S58 2026 | DDC 005.13--dc23

Published in 2026 by
Gareth Stevens Publishing
2544 Clinton St.
Buffalo, NY 14224

First published in Great Britain in 2023 by Wayland
Copyright © Hodder and Stoughton, 2023

Commissioning Editor: Grace Glendinning
Project Manager: Katie Woolley
Designer: Emma DeBanks
Illustrations: Dave Smith

The website addresses (URLs) included in this book were valid at the time of going to press. However, it is possible that contents or addresses may have changed since the publication of this book. No responsibility for any such changes can be accepted by either the author or the Publisher.

All rights reserved. No part of this book may be reproduced in any form without permission in writing from the publisher, except by a reviewer.

Printed in the United States of America

CPSIA compliance information: Batch #CSGS26: For further information contact Gareth Stevens at 1-800-542-2595.

CONTENTS

Screen-free Coding with Nature
4

What Is Coding?
6

Key Coding Concept #1: The Algorithm
8

Key Coding Concept #2: Sequence
9

Key Coding Concept #3: Loops
10

Key Coding Concept #4: Variables
11

Key Coding Concept #5: Branching
12

Key Coding Concept #6: Decomposition
13

Activity 1: Variables and Loops Unplugged: Code a Scavenger Hunt
14

Spot the Code!
22

Activity 2: Algorithms Unplugged: Code Your Own Treasure Map
24

Decompose This!
32

Activity 3: Branching Unplugged: If/Then Nature Activity
34

Spot the Bug!
42

Let's Solve a Coding Puzzle!
44

Glossary, Notes for Adults and Further Info
46

Answers
48

SCREEN-FREE CODING WITH NATURE

Let's go on a **CODING ADVENTURE** in **NATURE**! We're going to learn how to think like a computer with fun, nature-themed activities you can do wherever you call home.

The activities in this book are all **UNPLUGGED**, which means you don't need a computer or a screen to learn how to code. Most of the fun is made even better with a group, using teamwork as you explore nature and coding in the fresh air!

You won't believe how many coding concepts are at play as you work on scavenger hunts, nature walks, grouping animals, matching habitats, and more!

LET'S GET OUTDOORS AND LEARN TO CODE WITH NATURE!

WHAT IS CODING?

Coding means **TALKING** to computers in a language they understand. Computers aren't naturally smart! A computer doesn't understand what to do unless the instructions are written in "computer code."

If a computer is asked to **PLAN THE BEST NATURE HIKE**, it wouldn't automatically know how to do it.

WHAT **IS** A "NATURE HIKE"?

A computer would need to be told where to **START** and **FINISH**, where the walking trails are, which ones are open for exploring—and **MANY MORE DETAILS!**

KID CODERS

By the end of this book, you're going to be talking in "**COMPUTER SPEAK**" and will know how to give computers instructions that they will understand—no screen necessary.

CODING IN NATURE!
Did you know that coding is **EVERYWHERE**? We use coding to help us understand nature's cycles and systems, and nature itself uses lots of coding concepts every day.

KIDS CAN CODE TOO!
You don't have to be an expert to learn to code — there are **6 SIMPLE CODING CONCEPTS** that you can learn to get started with coding at any age.

CODING CONCEPTS
You may know some of these already, but you can turn the page to remind yourself, or use the next few pages as quick references when you start the nature **ACTIVITIES** later in the book.

KEY CODING CONCEPT #1: THE ALGORITHM

An **ALGORITHM** is an **INSTRUCTION** given to help complete a certain task.

We can think of it like the **CAREFUL DIRECTIONS** we need when we're visiting a new trail.

These directions form the algorithm that tells us how to get from your car to the beach.

Sometimes there is more than one way to get to where you're headed—there might be **"THE SCENIC ROUTE"** algorithm, or the **"FASTEST ROUTE"** algorithm.

On this map, for example, the **"SCENIC ROUTE"** algorithm would tell you to:

**GO 0.5 MILE (800 M) NORTH
THEN 0.5 MILE (800 M) EAST
THEN 0.25 MILE (400 M) NORTH AGAIN**

It's not the quickest route, but it takes you past a beautiful waterfall!

KEY CODING CONCEPT #2: SEQUENCE

SEQUENCE refers to the **ORDER** of steps in your algorithm.

The **ORDER** of **STEPS** is very important when completing a task.

Have you ever heard of the life cycle of a frog? When frogs go from eggs to tadpoles to froglets to frogs they are growing in a **CERTAIN SEQUENCE,** or **ORDER**.

The **LIFE CYCLES** of animals follow a **SPECIFIC SEQUENCE** that allows the animal to become fully grown. You can't go backwards from tadpole to egg!

KEY CODING CONCEPT #3:
LOOPS

A loop is a **SET** of **INSTRUCTIONS** that repeat and repeat until a specific condition is met.

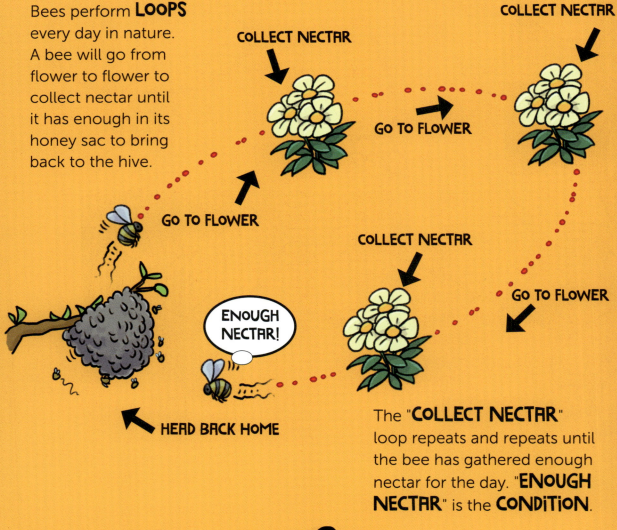

Bees perform **LOOPS** every day in nature. A bee will go from flower to flower to collect nectar until it has enough in its honey sac to bring back to the hive.

The "**COLLECT NECTAR**" loop repeats and repeats until the bee has gathered enough nectar for the day. "**ENOUGH NECTAR**" is the **CONDITION**.

KEY CODING CONCEPT #4: VARIABLES

A variable is a way of **HOLDING INFORMATION**. It's like a box that keeps information inside it.

Variables can be represented by **LETTERS**, **WORDS**, or **NUMBERS**.

In nature, we can sort living things according to their species. We can think of the word 'tree' as a variable and the different species of tree as the information held inside.

If you live in a tropical climate, you may have mostly palm trees in your "trees" variable. If you live in a colder climate, you may have mostly firs.

KEY CODING CONCEPT #5: BRANCHING

Branching refers to making a **DECISION** based on what is **HAPPENING** or has **HAPPENED**.

In nature, we often make decisions based on the weather. If it's sunny outside, we apply sunscreen. If it's raining outside, we bring an umbrella. If it's cold, we wear a hat and gloves.

These **DECISIONS** are **EXAMPLES** of a **BRANCH**.

KEY CODING CONCEPT #6: DECOMPOSITION

Decomposition refers to breaking something up into **SMALLER PARTS**.

Do you know how birds build their nests? It's quite a complicated process, but when we break it down, we can see that it involves a few **KEY STEPS**.

First birds will **DROP** twigs and sticks to make a base. Then they **WEAVE** grasses and leaves using their beaks. Some birds even use saliva or spiders' webs to **GLUE** their nest together!

TA-DA!

IT'S ACTIVITY TIME! →

Variables and Loops Unplugged: Code a Scavenger Hunt

Let's design an outdoor scavenger hunt, coding style!

In this activity we're going to put our knowledge of **VARIABLES** and **LOOPS** to the test. This activity is most fun done outside with a group of friends—screen-free in the fresh air!

 WARNING: Outdoor coders must be very careful and should have the permission and help of an adult when doing any activity.

MATERIALS YOU WILL NEED:

- 4 jars
- At least 24 small pieces of paper
- 1 large piece of paper
- Pen
- Die
- Adult to help

JARS

BITS OF PAPER

PAPER

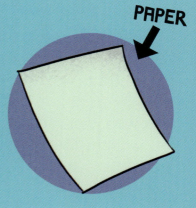

PEN

DIE

REMEMBER: DON'T DISTURB NATURE AS YOU HUNT—USE YOUR EYES ONLY TO SPOT EACH ITEM!

THANKS, **DAD!**

STEP ONE! CREATE YOUR VARIABLES

Remember that a **VARIABLE** is like a **CONTAINER** to **HOLD INFORMATION**. In this activity, you will create several containers to hold scavenger hunt ideas.

Start with your four jars and label each one with the following variables:

Now you need to come up with **IDEAS** (or **VALUES**) that you can store in the **VARIABLE JARS** that relate to that variable.

You'll need your creative brain to come up with a fun nature scavenger hunt list.

Write six nature hunt ideas for each variable on small pieces of paper and place them in each jar.

IDEAS for your hunt—add your own ideas if you wish!

TOUCH
- SOMETHING **PRICKLY**
- SOMETHING **SOFT**
- SOMETHING **LIQUID**
- SOMETHING **HARD**
- SOMETHING **ROUGH**
- SOMETHING **SQUISHY**

SMELL
- SOMETHING **SWEET**
- SOMETHING **STINKY**
- A **SMELL** YOU **LIKE**
- SOMETHING **ROTTEN**
- SOMETHING **FRESH**
- SOMETHING **ODORLESS**

SEE
- SOMETHING **RED** (OR ANOTHER COLOR)
- SOMETHING **TALLER** THAN YOU
- SOMETHING **SMALL**
- SOMETHING **COLORFUL**
- SOMETHING **BLACK**
- SOMETHING **PATTERNED**

HEAR
- THE **SOUND** OF THE **WIND**
- SOMETHING THAT **CRUNCHES**
- SOMETHING **LOUD**
- SOMETHING **BUZZING**
- SOMETHING **CHIRPING**
- SOMETHING **DRIPPING**

STEP TWO!
CODE YOUR LIST AND LOOP IT

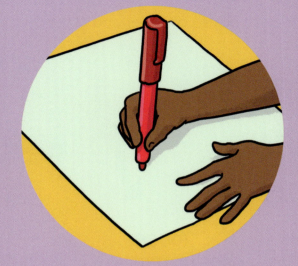

Now it's time to **CODE** your **SCAVENGER HUNT LIST**.

From each jar pull **THREE PIECES OF PAPER**. Write out these items on the large piece of paper to create your official scavenger hunt list.

ROLL your die to determine how many **LOOPS** (repeats) you will need for the two looping items.

FIND FOUR COLORFUL THINGS!

Select two items that you would like to **LOOP**. Remember a loop is something you **REPEAT**. For the items with a loop you will need to find more than one on your scavenger hunt!

Write how many **REPEATS** you need next to the item.

EXAMPLE

SCAVENGER HUNT LIST

TOUCH
Something prickly
Something soft x 6
Something liquid

SMELL
Something sweet
Something stinky
A smell you like

SEE
Something colorful x 4
Something black
Something patterned

SOUND
Something that crunches
Something loud
Something buzzing

GAME PLAY: LET'S GO HUNTING!

Now that you have created your scavenger hunt list it's time to go out into nature!

SEARCH for items that match the description on your **LIST** and check them off when you have seen them. If you have a **LOOP** don't forget that you'll need to check that item off more than once to meet your condition!

ALGORITHMS UNPLUGGED: CODE YOUR OWN TREASURE MAP

In this activity, we're going to get outside and follow a map to find some treasure! We'll also learn how to use a compass to give directions clearly.

In this activity you'll learn all about **ALGORITHMS** and how planning them precisely gets us to our goal —the treasure!

MATERIALS YOU MAY NEED:

* An air-tight container
* A special item to leave as treasure in the container (A few small coins or stickers will work. Don't use something edible or you may tempt some animals to steal the treasure!)
* A compass
* Pencil and paper
* Permission from an adult to bury your treasure!

GAME SET UP!

Start off by hiding your valuable item in its container somewhere **OUTSIDE**.

Be sure to get permission to bury or hide the container before you do!

Now pick a spot to start your treasure hunt—you can **MARK** the **STARTING POINT** with chalk or some sticks to make it super clear. The farther away from the treasure, the more **COMPLEX** your algorithm will be.

GRAB YOUR PEN AND PAPER. IT'S TIME TO COME UP WITH YOUR ALGORITHM!

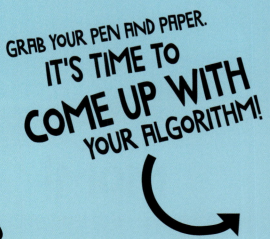

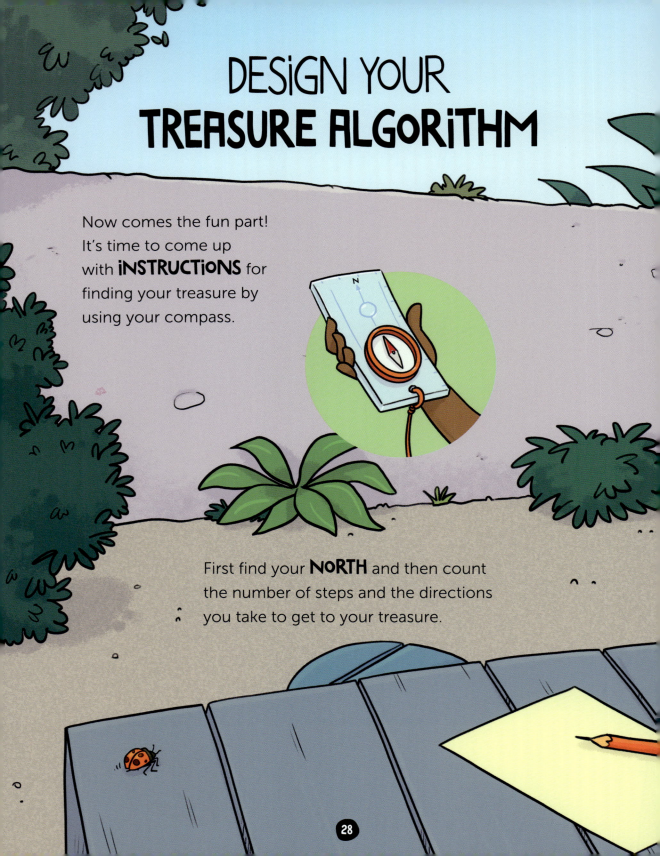

DESIGN YOUR TREASURE ALGORITHM

Now comes the fun part! It's time to come up with **INSTRUCTIONS** for finding your treasure by using your compass.

First find your **NORTH** and then count the number of steps and the directions you take to get to your treasure.

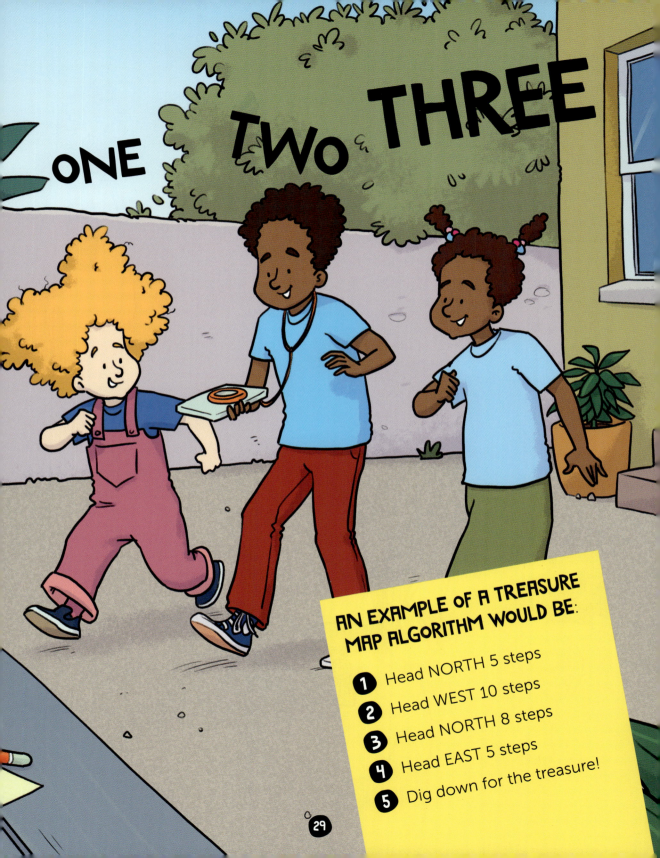

GAME PLAY: TEST YOUR ALGORITHM

Now it's time to **TEST** your algorithm. Find a parent, friend, or other trusted adult who doesn't know where you've hidden the treasure. Give them a copy of your treasure algorithm and take them to the starting spot.

From that spot they will need to **FOLLOW THE ALGORITHM** and see if they find the treasure!

DON'T FORGET TO DEBUG!

Made a mistake in your algorithm? Don't worry! Mistakes are **COMMON** in coding. Real-life coders call fixing mistakes in their code **DEBUGGING**.

If your algorithm doesn't turn out right the first time, you can simply debug the algorithm and set your treasure-hunter back on the **RIGHT PATH**.

DECOMPOSE THIS!

An ocean habitat has so many interesting animals and plants, all living together in a complicated system. Can you help **DECOMPOSE** this ocean scene by finding and listing all the different colors you can see in the amazing coral reef?

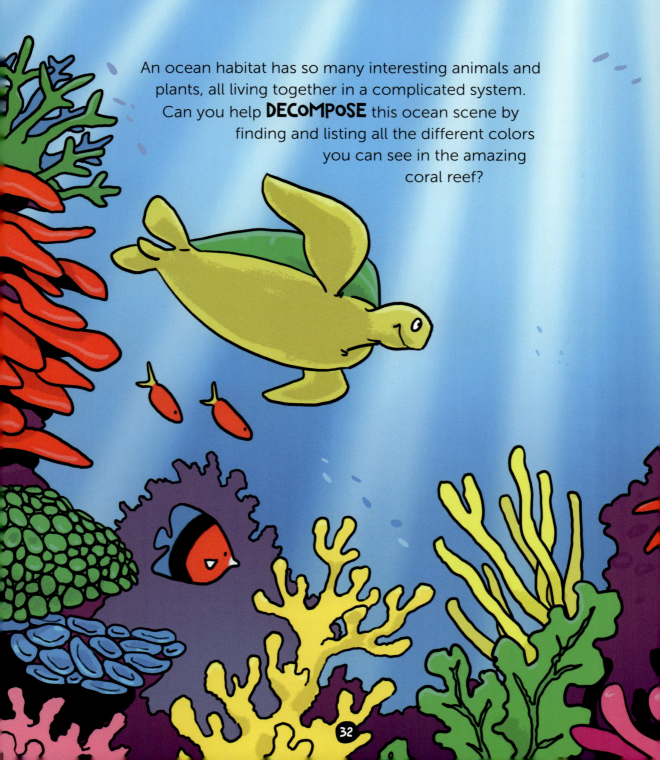

BRANCHING UNPLUGGED:
IF/THEN NATURE ACTIVITY

Let's play Red Light, Green Light with a twist! This nature activity will get you jumping, dancing, and enjoying the outdoors with friends.

In this activity, we will learn all about branching. Remember **BRANCHING** is making a **DECISION** based on what's going on.

When coders write branches they use **IF/THEN** statements.

IF IT'S RAINING OUTSIDE ➡ THEN BRING AN UMBRELLA.

IF IT'S COLD OUTSIDE ➡ THEN WEAR A COAT.

➡ NOW WE'RE GOING TO USE THESE IDEAS TO CREATE OUR OWN FUN GAME! ➡

MATERIALS YOU WILL NEED:

* Different colored leaves and other natural objects
* An open area to play

1. They should be things already fallen/on the ground.
2. You should return them to the ground in a safe place when done.

LEAVES

NATURAL OBJECTS

DON'T FORGET TO GET **PERMISSION** FROM AN ADULT BEFORE YOU GO OUT INTO NATURE, AND **BEFORE** YOU TOUCH OR MOVE ANYTHING!

GAME SET UP!

Start by gathering **THREE OR FOUR NATURE ITEMS** that can easily be held in your hand.

EXAMPLES:

RED LEAF

GREEN LEAF

PINE CONE

SMALL ROCK

Now it's time to "**PROGRAM**" our items with **IF/THEN** statements.

Come up with an **IF/THEN** statement for each object. You can use these examples below or come up with your own ideas!

EXAMPLES

IF I hold up a red leaf, **THEN** you jump up and down on the spot.

IF I hold up a pine cone, **THEN** you freeze.

IF I hold up a green leaf, **THEN** you run forwards.

IF I hold up a rock, **THEN** you do a dance move.

GAME PLAY:

Now it's time to play your game!

1 One player is the **"PROGRAMMER."** Make sure all your nature objects are within reach of this player.

2 Have all the other players start at a **STARTING LINE** away from the programmer.

3 The programmer begins the game by holding up an **OBJECT**.

OBJECT

IF GREEN, THEN RUN!

4 Players need to follow the **IF/THEN** statement assigned to that item.

5 Mistakes are a normal part of coding. If a player makes a mistake following their **IF/THEN** statement, then the programmer shouts **"BUG!"** and that player will need to take five steps backwards to **DEBUG** their algorithm.

6 The first player to reach the programmer **WINS!**

Now, let's play it again! Choose a new player to be the programmer. For extra creativity you can even change your branches so that there are new actions for each of your objects.

SPOT THE BUG!

The water cycle is the path that water follows as it travels all around the globe. Can you find the sequencing error here?

← PRECIPITATION

COLLECTION

LET'S SOLVE A CODING PUZZLE!

We've now learned the basic concepts of coding and you are ready to think just like a computer.

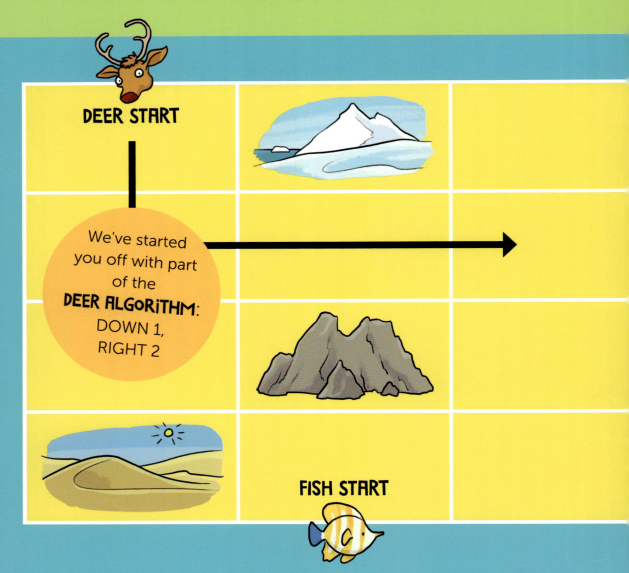

(ANSWERS ON PAGE 48)

In this puzzle, we'll need to use our coding skills to solve a habitat maze.

 Help each animal find its way to its habitat. You will have to code four animal algorithms to finish this puzzle!

 Write out the algorithms on a separate piece of paper.

CAMEL START

POLAR BEAR START

THINK LIKE A COMPUTER!

GLOSSARY

ALGORITHM:
An algorithm is an instruction given to help complete a certain task.

BRANCH:
Branching refers to making a decision based on what is happening or has happened.

CONDENSATION:
Condensation is the process of water vapor changing back to liquid. This is how clouds form.

DEBUG:
When you debug, you find and solve a problem in coding instructions.

DECOMPOSITION:
Decomposition means breaking down problems into smaller steps.

EVAPORATION:
Evaporation is the process of a liquid turning into a gas.

LOOP:
A loop is a set of instructions that repeat until a specific condition is met.

PRECIPITATION:
Precipitation describes the process of water falling to Earth in the form of rain, snow, or hail.

SEQUENCE:
Sequence refers to the order of steps.

VARIABLE:
A variable is a way of holding information. It's like a box that keeps information inside it.

NOTES FOR ADULTS

WHY CODING UNPLUGGED?

Teaching kids to code is a great way to introduce them to the basics of programming and have them learn problem-solving, logic, and critical thinking skills. These skills are applicable in real life, in school, at work, or even while they're playing video games!

One of the best ways to begin coding is to learn to code **UNPLUGGED**, so no computer or other hardware is required! By taking coding offline, it's easy to focus on the basic concepts, which are fundamental to learning to code. Combining coding learning with creative or physical activities is a great way to embed the information and keep children active.

FURTHER INFO

FOR MORE FUN CODING BOOKS, WHY NOT TRY ...

Briggs, Jason R. *Python for Kids: A Playful Introduction to Programming*. San Francisco, CA: No Starch Press, 2023.

Vale, Jenna. *Get Coding with Scratch*. Buffalo, NY: Gareth Stevens Publishing, 2024.

ANSWERS:

PAGE 23:
For example: The boy planning his route is creating an algorithm.
The girl tying her shoe is performing a sequence.
The woodpecker is performing a loop.
The ants are performing an algorithm, which they loop until they have met their food-gathering condition for the day!
The sign posts create a branch for walkers to choose a direction.

PAGE 33:
Red, orange, blue, purple, pink, yellow, black, white, and green

PAGE 43:
The evaporation arrows should be facing up toward the cloud.

PAGE 45: EXAMPLE ALGORITHMS

Deer Algorithm
Down 1
Right 2
Down 2
Right 1

Camel Algorithm
Down 2
Left 2
Down 1
Left 2

Polar Bear Algorithm
Down 1
Left 1
Down 1
Left 2
Up 2
Left 1

Fish Algorithm
Right 1
Up 1
Right 2
Down 1
Right 1